How We Did It

How We Did It

A Story of How a Single Mother
Raised a Special-Needs Child

Tascha L. Stith

BALBOA.
PRESS

A DIVISION OF HAY HOUSE

ISBN: 978-1-4525-5063-3 (sc)
ISBN: 978-1-4525-5061-9 (hc)
ISBN: 978-1-4525-5062-6 (e)

Balboa Press books may be ordered through booksellers or by contacting:

Balboa Press
A Division of Hay House
1663 Liberty Drive
Bloomington, IN 47403
www.balboapress.com
1-(877) 407-4847

Photos on cover and page 83 taken by Nolan Conley Photography
Line editing done by Mikki George

Printed in the United States of America

Library of Congress Control Number: 2012907151

Balboa Press rev. date: 5/04/2012

Additional copyright information

Contents

DEDICATION

· · · · · ·

To the one who has inspired me, made me better and helped me to understand. For all the pain, the tears, the hard work, the suffering, the sleepless nights, and the joy, it was all worth it to see who you have become today! I dedicate this book to the joy of my life, my beautiful daughter JASMINE. We did this together, you and me, and I love you with all my heart.

ACKNOWLEDGMENTS

• • • • • • • • • • •

To the One who has shined such a light upon my life, whose arms I felt encamped around me on my darkest days. To the one and only living GOD who has been constant, steady, loving and patient every day of my life. Who said "for such a time as this," has given me guidance, strength, and the heart to write such a book. You knew my life the day it was created. I faltered and I made mistakes; but You have always been there no matter what, and I am so glad to know You!

To Valerie Hart, words can never express the love I have for you and your family. You loved us from the day we met fifteen years ago. You have stood the test of time with me. There has never been a time when we could not count on you. I remember Typhany watching Jasmine at four years old. I remember Boris picking her up and carrying her into the house so that snow would not get on her while getting out of the car. I will never ever forget the love, joy, and peace you all have brought to our lives. You are my BEST friend; you are Mama Pudding. I love you with all my heart.

To Keith Williams, oh my, what a journey! We met when Jasmine was just three months old. Who knew that because of our love for bowling, we would be friends today? You knew my dad before you knew me. He brought his baby girl, a left-hander who barely understood the game, to a bowling center and the rest is history. It just goes to show you never know who you will meet. Thank you for being in our lives. Thank you for loving us enough to understand our pain and our struggles and for being there always. You are the best and I will never forget you.

To Michael Morgan, Wow! How do I even describe you? The one who said write it down, put it on paper. You allowed me to bend your ear with worry and doubt, but you never stopped praying. You have helped me in so many ways. You have been a friend, an encourager, an awesome man of God. You have believed in me and have given me wisdom, guidance, a listening ear, and a voice. Thank You! I can truly say you are my friend. I feel like I have known you all my life. Continue to do good works, good deeds, and keep on being you. I love you to pieces and I wish nothing but the best for you always. If you ever need me, you know I am there.

To the Veal family, there are so many of you that I cannot name you all; but Liz, you have been a second mom to me. You stepped right in there and you helped me with Jazz. You loved her and me. You made us family. We definitely felt like we were a part of the family. Each one of you made that happen. Thank you. We will never forget you. Robbin, I love ya girl. Sheila, Mamie, ML... thanks to all of you!

To Cynthia Williams, you told me, "Stop doing everything and make her, she can do it. You are going to make yourself sick." You looked me dead in my face and said, "I am not trying to hurt you, but Jasmine is slick, she can do this, but you have to let her." I will never forget those words; you helped me and prepared me for the journey. You are amazing, funny, and I love you always.

There are so many people... doctors, hospitals and nurses that cared and helped us to become who we are today. Thank you all.

To my confidants, thank you for having that listening ear. Thank you for still being here. The name is so fitting because you never judged, you listened, you helped, and you were there; and that was enough. I love you all!

PREFACE

· · · · ·

Where do I start was the question. It took months just to get this part started. I had written several chapters before even realizing that I was writing a book. One night I just started writing and before you knew it, I was on this path.

I never had any idea that our lives would become so public. Never in my life did I imagine that one day I would be sharing the life of a parent with a special needs child.

On this journey called life, we are called to do things that make absolutely no sense to us. One night not too long ago, I was sleeping and dreaming; and my dream, simply put, was about forgiveness. I had to forgive all those who I felt had done wrong by me. The dream was so clear. It went something like this: how can you tell a story if you have not forgiven those who you felt have done wrong by you. I had no idea what that meant. Then it dawned on me that a book is a story; and when you open it up you are prepared to read it, analyze it, and use it in some sort of way to help you. Whether it is just for your reading pleasure, your studies, or maybe some form of inspiration, it's being used for some purpose. It is my hope that this book will be used to help someone.

INTRODUCTION

• • • • • • • • •

I was twenty-four years old, pregnant, married, and in a matter of months, separated. I lived in Virginia when I first found out I was pregnant, I thought my husband would be happy to start a family with me. Never in my wildest dreams did I think he would look at me and tell me he didn't want a child with me. Even worse, he didn't want to be married to me anymore. He felt we should have lived together before getting married. Can you say, "It's a little too late for that?" I was shocked; I honestly thought he loved me, considering that he asked me to marry him and placed a ring on my finger.

At the time, he was still in the military, and just after two months of marriage, he got deployed to Iraq in April of 1993. We communicated while he was away, but nothing changed. I continued to believe that he would come home and the marriage would work itself out. Boy was I wrong; he came home in July and was still speaking the same language, divorce! I packed up all my things, and at five and half months pregnant, I left. He and his uncle moved me back to my hometown in Ohio. We barely spoke after that, and when we did, we argued all the time. It was horrible. I went to all my doctor's appointments by myself, and I was preparing to do this alone. What I was not prepared for was having a sickly baby; this is where our journey begins.

CHAPTER 1

. . . .

Nine Months

NINE months seems like a lifetime when you are pregnant. Your feet swell, they hurt, and you are tired and sleepy all the time. Your belly is growing at a rapid speed, and your body is changing every single day. Your face is shining bright, and you have this aura about you. Your hormones are all over the place, and you cry at the drop of a dime; when I say *everything* is happening, I mean *everything.* You spend more time in the bathroom than you've ever spent—you could have gone literally five minutes ago, but as soon as you get done, you're right back there again.

It's so amazing to look back at all you go through when you're pregnant. But what most people don't know is that you also go through other things that aren't all that exciting. I remember waking up one morning unable to walk because my baby had decided that she needed a more comfortable position. Although it was the most painful feeling to me, it sure was not to her. I had to go to the doctor so they could reposition her because she was sitting on my pelvis. Imagine that.

Pregnancy has been regarded as the most exciting thing you could ever experience, but this isn't true for everyone. I was stressed and sad most of the time. I was not looking forward to being a single parent, and I had no idea how I was going to do it. I had just relocated to Ohio; I was unemployed temporarily and living at home with my mother. That's no way to start your family. This was especially hard because I had served in the military, so I hadn't lived at home since I was seventeen. But there I was, back at home. I was fortunate enough to obtain a job with the state of Ohio. I truly believe they thought I was just fat and had no idea I was pregnant or within ninety days of giving birth. I don't believe they would have hired me if they had known.

I moved out of my mother's house into my own apartment right before giving birth. I went shopping and started making plans for the day I would become a mom. This was exciting—all of the cute clothes, all the different types of bottles, all the baby toys, the cute beds and blankets. Everything was so pretty, but something told me to buy all neutral colors. I didn't know the sex of the baby, and I didn't want to know—I wanted it to be a surprise. I started picking out names for both girls and boys.

Then, reality set in. I was sitting on the couch, and my belly did the wave. I watched my belly move up and down and sideways, and it became more and more apparent that it would not be long before the little person inside of me would be here. I sat there in amazement. My belly got hard on one side. I looked lopsided because the baby had decided to find a more comfortable position and stick his or her butt out. So, on one side I had this hard bulge. I called my mom and asked her why my belly was looking like that. She felt my belly and said, "Girl, that's the baby's butt." Sure enough, when I went to the doctor the next morning, it was the baby's butt. It had turned itself into the breach position and had pushed its butt to my left side. I had some time before giving birth, so he wasn't that concerned. He believed the baby would turn around, and it did, but boy was that uncomfortable.

He also informed me that I was doing well, considering that early in my pregnancy I was diagnosed with placenta previa. This is very dangerous because it can cause miscarriage; my pregnancy was then considered high risk. I have to assume that it corrected itself on its own. I am not a doctor, so I only give you the facts as they were given to me.

CHAPTER 2

. . . .

Here Comes a Baby!

I woke up one morning and had to go to another doctor's appointment. Because I was getting closer to my due date, my appointments were weekly. However, when I went to the bathroom, I was bleeding. I was at my mom's house, and I called out for her and asked her if I was supposed to be bleeding. She said, "No, you are in labor." This would explain why I was so uncomfortable all night and barely slept. The bleeding is called "show" or "bloody show;" it is a sign that the cervix has dilated somewhat and the onset of labor is imminent.

I got dressed and went to my doctor's appointment, and sure enough, I was in labor, with my contractions about eight to ten minutes apart. They monitored me for a while, then sent me home and told me to come back when my contractions where about three to five minutes apart. No one ever told me it would take thirty-one hours.

I went back to the hospital later that day, but I had only dilated one centimeter, so they sent me back home again. I went back to the hospital several hours later. I was tired from walking all day and waiting. The nurse came in to see me, but she did something strange. She gave me this little red pill to help me rest. She told me it was going to be awhile because I was now only two centimeters. She also told me that this pill would not affect the baby, but that I needed to sleep because it was going to be a long night, and she sent me home again.

This process was taking quite a long time! I ended up back in the hospital that night, and that little red pill she gave me was not doing a thing—nothing to me, at least. Thirty-one hours later, it's November 25, 1993, Thanksgiving Day! She arrived at 7:02 a.m. She weighed five pounds, three ounces and was nineteen inches long. She had all ten fingers and toes. She had the most beautiful hair and eyes. She was the most beautiful thing I had ever seen. You could literally hold her in one hand like a five-pound bag of sugar.

She just looked at me and I looked at her, and I didn't know what to do, what to feel. I knew absolutely nothing. She did not have a book, a manual, an instruction certificate, or anything like that with her. They took her away to clean her up and check her out. While they were tending to her, something was wrong with me. They couldn't stop the bleeding. I remember dozing on and off as they worked on me for a while. I guess that pill had started working.

Finally, they got me together and took me to my room, where I passed out. I was exhausted; I had been in labor for thirty-one hours and it had kicked my butt. I saw her for a little while, but they wanted me to rest, and I wanted to rest. Now I have heard people say they didn't want the nurses or doctors to take their babies out of the room, but it wasn't that way for me. They took her, and I was relieved. Have you ever heard of "baby blues" or postpartum depression? I was already experiencing it. "The difficulty bonding with my baby and the sadness were signs that it was affecting me."

I was somewhat detached. I couldn't breastfeed, although I tried, she had a problem with the sucking technique even with a bottle. I suppose that should have been the first sign, but I did not know any better. They continued to try to get me to breastfeed; they tried the breast pump as well. I started to bleed from my nipples, so that was not going to work. They cleaned me up, using warm compresses to relieve the pain, but all that did was cause my breast to leak milk and hurt even more. You would think if she was not latching on to the breast, she'd take a bottle, but that didn't work either. We ended up staying in the hospital for a few extra days.

Just as we were getting ready to check out, the nurse who had been with me all night came to my room. At the time, this didn't seem strange. She was wonderful and had taken care of my baby and me for several hours. It later dawned on me that these people see women deliver babies twenty-four hours a day, seven days a week, 365 days a year. So what made my baby and me so special? Did she know something had gone wrong during my delivery? When I discovered that something was wrong with Jasmine, I requested my medical records only to find that there were missing pages. It became apparent that mine was not a normal delivery. I discovered that my baby had lost oxygen for over ten minutes. Also, I was rushed from the birthing room to the delivery room, which was more like an EMERGENCY room.

The birthing room was set up for me to deliver my baby right there. There were monitors, the stirrups for my feet, the whole shebang. The doctor would come in often to monitor my dilation progress. The nurses prepped me and made sure I was ready when the time came. I was sure I was going to deliver right there. They had prepared this room and even told me it wouldn't be long—that they just wanted to make sure I was fully dilated (that would be 10 centimeters). The delivery room, by contrast, should be called the EMERGENCY room. In this room, I went from being prepped for delivery, to being turned on all fours like a dog.

I believe this is when my pregnancy became even more complicated. I was in so much pain that I agreed to have an epidural; I could not take it anymore. From that moment on, things changed and they changed rapidly. Do I believe it was because of the epidural? Not necessarily. I'm just stating the facts as they occurred. Since I was there, who knows better than me? Why do I believe that? Prior to the epidural, I was in labor, and had been there for a long time. However, as soon as I got the epidural, everything changed. They started putting this buzzing horn-like thing on my stomach to get a response from the baby. She would come down and then go back up. They told me she was falling asleep and had to be wakened (remember that little red pill that wasn't supposed to affect my baby—that would be the first lie).

My water broke within minutes of the epidural; everything started to feel chaotic to me. The relaxing, calm environment became panicked. My cousin was put out of the birthing room, and I was rushed to the delivery room. I remember my cousin crying hysterically and asking questions. She wanted to know why and where they were taking us, and if we were going to be all right. She already had two children of her own, so it was obvious to her that something was wrong. Why else would she be panicking?

I remember telling the nurse I have to push. She said, "Don't, not yet." Then she smiled and said, "Everything is going to be all right." I told her I felt like I had to go to the bathroom; she said, "Oh, this is going to be the best bowel movement you will ever have." I didn't know why she said that. I also did not know that when having a baby, you could have a bowel movement right there on the table. The next thing I remember was seeing my cousin, and hearing her telling me how beautiful my baby was. It seemed as though I was in some kind of fog. Once I got into that delivery room everything was happening so fast.

I got to my room and slept for a while. When they brought her in later, I was told that she had a little jaundice and they wanted to keep her under the light. I saw my family later that day. They brought me Thanksgiving dinner and sweet potato pie. That was Thanksgiving for us!

CHAPTER 3

· · · · · · · ·

When did I know?

THE truth is, I didn't know. There was something that my dad said to me. He said, "Whatever you do, you take care of this baby." Well, hell Dad, what did you think I was going to do? I may have been young, but you have always said that I was responsible, and that you were proud of my accomplishments. I hadn't accomplished anything compared to this! The truth is, my dad knew something was wrong! He died when my daughter was two and a half years old, and his wife later told me that he was worried from the first day he saw Jasmine.

Why would he be worried? She didn't look different. There was nothing wrong with her. Or, was I in denial? Looking back, I believe I *was* in denial. I truly don't know, but I do know that by the time she was able to see and focus, she was very cross-eyed.

Her beautiful eyes had turned toward her nose; this was the first sign. She wasn't crawling, she wasn't sitting up on her own, and she was barely making "goo goo gaa gaa" noises. She was several months behind in her development, according to the timetable charts for babies. She mostly smiled and played with her feet. If it weren't for my aunt telling me to get out of denial and find out what was going on with this baby, I believe I would have stayed there—lost, confused, and working myself into a tizzy.

She was crying all the time. I was up all hours of the night, calling everyone I knew, thinking she had colic. I gave her water with a dash of lemon-lime soda, and a little baking soda. It was an old school remedy from my grandmother. I took all the advice from everyone I knew with children. Still not wanting to believe, see, or realize that something was wrong.

Then the doctor's visits began. I spent more time at the hospitals than I did eating or sleeping. She had multiple ear infections; the doctors tried every antibiotic available. This went on forever, and then came the threat of death. They didn't know what was wrong, but she was severely ill. When she was seven months old, she was diagnosed with Coxsackie Virus. Her temperature was 104 degrees and rising. The doctors initially thought it was another ear infection and put her on more antibiotics. Two days later, she had a temperature of 105 degrees and we were back in the emergency room. But this time we were admitted.

The doctors said we needed to get her temperature down; if it rose to 106 degrees, it would be life threatening. I was freaking out. We had been there shortly before, and the doctors said it was just another ear infection! This was when we were told about the Coxsackie virus and placed in isolation. I was told it was life threatening, and no one could see her except me. I had to wear sterilized clothing while in her room, so I wouldn't transmit any germs. She later developed a red rash all over her body, and that's when she started to get better. In reality, her body was fighting the virus. She had several more ear infections, plus eye surgery by the time she was 0 months.

I have never been given a definitive diagnosis of what made her sick. I remember going to my OB/GYN appointment when I was thirty-seven weeks pregnant. The doctor, who wasn't my regular physician, said to me, "Are you sure your baby is due in November?" I said, "That's what they have always told me." He said, "He doesn't appear to be getting any bigger. If he doesn't come on the date they say, don't let them induce your labor. He will come when he is ready, and I want to see him get bigger." Yes, I said "him." They said she was a boy. Can you see I knew absolutely nothing? I just listened to everything those doctors told me. I say this because once Jasmine was here things changed.

I stopped taking advice from others. I did some digging and found the best doctors in their fields, because I demanded it and my child deserved it! I wanted to know what qualified them to treat and diagnosis my daughter. I wouldn't see doctors who were residents, because they were still in training; and I understand that they grow and perfect themselves through training, but not with my daughter.

Jasmine continued to get one ear infection after another. The antibiotics were not working, and the only thing they could tell me was that she was just behind, but that she would catch up. No one knew what was wrong with her. She was a beautiful little girl, smiling and happy. The only problem that anyone could see was that she wasn't doing things that babies her age were supposed to do. She was very small for her weight, and she has stayed in the forty percentile for the majority of her life. Due to all the medications she was on, she wasn't eating much. Side note here—when you read the labels on the medications listing all the side effects, believe them!

Ninety percent of the people suffer side effects of taking medications—one of them being loss of appetite—and Jasmine was no exception. She hardly ate, mostly because she was sleeping all the time— drowsiness was yet another side effect. My point here is that the doctors do not know everything. I'm not taking shots at those who have spent their lives studying medicine, but it's the truth. All I am saying is no one will know your child better than you, because you see it all. The doctors only see the children when you take them to clinics, or emergency rooms. This is to say that sometimes your instinct—that little voice—tells you something. Do not ignore it and don't let denial cause you to ignore your parental instincts. When you see or feel something is wrong, don't wait! Demand someone to listen to you, because your baby's life depends on it.

CHAPTER 4

· · · · · · · ·

The Diagnosis

THEY still don't know, and we've all heard of Autism Spectrum Disorder, Down Syndrome, Cerebral Palsy and a host of others. Have you ever heard of **Developmentally Delayed with Mental Retardation, Multiple Handicap with Epilepsy Seizure Disorder**? Well, this has its own category, and it's classified as non-specific (NOS), meaning it's not in one of the categories I listed above. The doctors believe it is caused by a lack of oxygen during birth, and this is what happened to Jasmine. She's also been diagnosed with Attention Deficit Hyperactivity Disorder (ADHD/ADD).

In some ways, I am glad to have not been given a definitive diagnosis, because I've heard the horror stories about insurance companies and their unwillingness to cover certain conditions. So far, I haven't experienced that problem. By the time Jasmine was ten years old, she had been in and out of hospitals so much that she should have a hospital named after her.

By sixteen months, she had already undergone bilateral eye surgery to correct her Strabismus condition. This is when both eyes cannot be directed at the same object at the same time, also known as cross-eyed. She was later diagnosed with Amblyopia as well. This is considered a lazy eye, so there are times that she appears to be looking out of her peripheral vision or looking at you sideways. We tried glasses to strengthen her eyes, but she didn't need them and wouldn't keep them on anyway. As a matter of fact, she broke the first pair.

She eventually had bilateral foot and ankle surgery to correct her residual club foot. They had to release the tendon cords in her ankles because they were so tight—with no give or elasticity—which is partly the reason she walks with a stiff gait. She was later diagnosed with mild Cerebral Palsy and Attention Deficit Hyperactivity Disorder. In 2003 she had what's called an Epilepsy Brain Resection to repair the damaged part of her brain and to control her seizures.

We spent a lot of time in and out of hospitals, clinics, and doctor's offices. They ran so many tests, including genetics chromosome testing, x-rays, MRIs, CAT scans, blood work. You name it, we did it. We did sleep studies where they would monitor her brain wave pattern as she slept. I'm telling you, Jasmine hated it. She didn't want to go to the doctors, she cried, she whined, she would wet her clothes. She was a nervous wreck. Every time I said we have to go to the doctors today, it would turn into a disaster. So I tried not telling her, thinking I would just drive there, we would get out the car, and it would be okay. As soon as we pulled into the parking lot she would start crying. She knew the building and she knew where we were. She would wet her clothes and not want to get out the car.

It took forever to get her to calm down and by forever I mean at least two years. That's why I say the doctors you choose are so important because they helped me with that. Slowly but surely she started to communicate and interact with the doctors. She would talk to them as best she could. They would let her put on gloves and hold the stethoscope up to their chest like she was listening to their heart. They made her comfortable and treated her like a person, not a person with a disability. They had what I call good bedside manners. THIS IS VERY IMPORTANT!

CHAPTER 5

· · · · · · · ·

It's Never Easy!

IF you allow someone to tell you that this is easy, that you won't feel pain, I am telling you right now that's a FLAT OUT lie! Stop listening to them, because they're allowing you to be in denial, and they're not helping you to get the help you need. It isn't because they don't love or care about you, but one thing I am sure of is that they absolutely do not know. Also, no one wants to be the one to tell you that something may be wrong with your baby; but they are hurting you by not telling you the truth.

Research is easy nowadays. You have at your disposal the internet, the library, early childhood intervention, etc. We are at a time in history where we can find out more than we want to know. I printed articles and used a whole lot of paper. If I read anything about symptoms that were the same as what I had seen in Jasmine,

I printed it and started asking questions. Could it be this or that? I read more articles, and kept a notebook of her symptoms. I got articles from the hospitals on what to look for, and what your baby should be doing in stages. I went to work! In 1993 there was less information available than there is today. This is because more and more of our children are being born with Autism, Cerebral Palsy, Epilepsy, Developmental Delays, and Mental Retardation. You name it, it's out there, and the information is readily available.

I was tired and exhausted. I slept in three hour increments. Why three hour increments? Because usually I was up already, considering she was sick all the time. So when she woke up, I woke up; and most times when she went to sleep, I was still up. I was afraid to sleep. I had worked myself into a panic. Remember, I was told that I was suffering from Post-Partum Depression (PPD), so I was also on medications to help me. Now I want everyone to know this is my opinion. That stuff makes you worse. You can't focus, you don't sleep and you're always tired. Because you're taking the medications, you make it through; but it seems to me that it's just a way to cloud your head even more, and fool you into thinking that you're thinking clearer. How can that be when you're always crying? How in the hell are you thinking clearer? And please don't tell me that crying purifies the soul, because I am here to tell you that this type of crying had nothing to do with that. This crying was out of frustration, lack of sleep, worry, and no help.

Over the years I have had the opportunity to talk with some other parents and compare notes. Even if you're married, it still requires a team effort, and if your spouse is not actively helping you then you need to sit down with him or her and tell them to get out of DENIAL. You have to do all you can with all your heart to work together for the sake of the child. The saying "teamwork makes a dream work" is so true.

I did all this on my own. I had no family and Jasmine's father wasn't around. I kept her away from most people because I didn't want her getting sick. You had to wash your hands and take off your shoes when you came over to my house. It was all about Jasmine. Most people didn't want to go through that, so they stayed away, and that was fine with me. The less the better, and I was tired of explaining.

As far as family goes, just because you are born into it doesn't mean you belong to it. You may have their genes, you may even have their last name, but what does that mean? This is not to offend anyone, it's just the truth. What do I mean by that? My daughter was not made by me alone. It takes two to tangle, and we can't force parents, grandparents, aunts, uncles, cousins, siblings, etc., to be active in our children's lives. If it's in their hearts, they will do what they can to help. I have never begged anyone to help, and everyone knew she was here. Every one of her relatives knew what her condition was, so those were the choices that they all made.

You just have to decide, not *if* it's going to affect you, but how you're going to keep it from affecting you, because it will. You'll feel alone, you'll get angry, you may even lash out; but I'm here to tell you, think about that baby! Be the best you for your child and for yourself (I wish someone had told me this, but if they had I probably would never have written this book). At the end of the day, everyone needs to be able to lay their head on their pillow and sleep. You can't control what people do, be it friends, family, or whoever. You can only control what you do for you and your baby.

When Jasmine was about to have her first eye surgery, I was sitting in church and I remember asking the pastor to say a prayer for us because surgery was the next day, and he did. I remember this lady whom I had never met before. She was an older lady full of wisdom, and she said to me, "It takes a Special Person to raise a Special Child." At first I didn't understand, but the closer I became to my Savior, the more I understood what she meant. I have kept those words with me from the time Jasmine was eight months old. Now she's eighteen. And she is fearfully and wonderfully made! No, this is not easy; but it is doable.

CHAPTER 6

· · · · · · · · ·

What To Do Now?

I sit here at 1:00 am reminded that a friend told me to write it down and "do not be afraid," and I think back on all the years I *was* afraid. I had no idea what or where this journey called life would take me. Would I be able to make it? Why me? How do I take the next step? Then I'm reminded of the little girl who comes and kisses me every single morning, waving and smiling. She says, "Good morning ma!" That is how I made it. That is how she made it. She knew that every day I was there to say good morning. We are there for each other! Don't be fooled into believing that some days weren't hard. Don't think that I did not cry, weep, blame, because I did. However, I also learned; and that is when you are on your way—when you learn. Learning is a big part of the journey.

There is an old saying, "each one, teach one." As I grew, so did Jasmine.

Around the age of three, Jasmine was napping on the couch. I looked over and she was jerking around. I had never seen this before. It took me about a minute or two to get her to respond to me. I gathered her up and went rushing to the emergency room. They just told me to keep an eye on her. It sounded like I described a seizure, but since she was fine now there was no way of knowing for sure. Great! I have no idea what had just happened. Well, two days later I was sure Jasmine had started having seizures. There were blank stares, falling down, daziness, complex partial seizures, and then generalized tonic-clonic seizures, also known as Grand-mal. This is when the body turns to one side, becomes stiff, and trembles uncontrollably. Also, it looks as if one is going to choke, eyes rolling to the back of the head, and loss of consciousness. Before I knew it, she was on more medications and having at least ten seizures a day.

CHAPTER 7

· · · · · · · ·

Epilepsy Seizure Disorder

L ET's talk about the seizures. They were grueling. I couldn't sleep, and Jasmine had started to sleep with me because I could not leave her alone, even though she wanted to sleep in her room. In addition, when she did sleep in her room I paced all night long. When I closed my eyes, I could feel my bed shaking even though she was not there. I knew from all my research that every time she had a seizure, it was doing more and more damage to her brain.

She wasn't gaining any weight because she hardly ate. It was so bad that my own mother told me she was afraid to watch over her. There were times I had to pull over because she would be in the back seat having a seizure. I remember sitting in my car just crying, feeling helpless. I would drive and stare in my rearview mirror, afraid to turn the music up too loud. If I wasn't looking in the mirror I was afraid I would hear this smacking sound, then look back and find her seizing. I would pull off the road when it was twenty below outside, snow everywhere; all that mattered was stopping the car and taking care of Jasmine. What else could I do? I couldn't stop the seizures; all I could do was make sure she didn't get hurt while having one.

I will never forget the day the security company came to my house to install the television monitors and cameras. I felt like some paranoid freak. I was paying all this money to have a television and monitor installed in each room of the house. It was impossible for me to be with her every second of the day. I still had responsibilities; I still needed to cook, clean, do laundry etc. I knew I couldn't continue to function as I had been doing—running up and down the stairs every time I heard the slightest noise. I was running myself into the ground. So I had cameras installed which enabled me to watch her when she was not in my presence. It truly helped me a lot.

I remember taking Jazz to the circus. I thought she would like it, but to my surprise not only did she not like it, but she had a seizure when we left. It was too loud for her. It didn't matter what the animals and the ring dancers were doing. The noise bothered her, and it also triggered another seizure. To this day, we do not go to amusement parks, circuses, or anything like that. I found there were all kinds of things she could not tolerate because they would cause seizures. She couldn't tolerate bright lights, flickering

Christmas tree lights or even loud noises. We made all kinds of adjustments and she was never allowed to be alone in the shower or tub.

It was hard because finding a sitter was damn near impossible, and when I did find them I kept them at any cost! When you have a sick child, no one wants to watch them; so when you find someone you trust, and whom your child likes, you keep them.

After three years and no answers, several CAT scans and MRIs later, I found a doctor who specialized in epilepsy. I researched and went through several doctors, but the blessing came when I moved to Cleveland, Ohio and found Rainbows Babies and Children's Hospital. This hospital is amazing. They never gave up, they listened to me, and they ran every single test they could to help me find out why she was having the seizures. I couldn't accept the fact that she had epilepsy. I questioned why she had it and what is causing it. If a question came to me I asked, even when they told me not to worry about it. I would say "NO, you answer me. I want to know everything." Rainbows Babies and Children's Hospital gave me the answers I needed!

Jasmine got a service dog named Emily. She was a working dog from Canine Assistants. We had attended the training, and she helped me with Jasmine. The dog would alert me if anything was not right with Jasmine. Of course she was well trained, and she stayed with Jazz no matter what. Emily was not allowed to go to school with her because Jasmine was not able to control her—and you have to be able to control your service dog. The problem was that there was no way to stop kids from wanting to pet and play with her, so Emily stayed home with me during the day. She knew when Jasmine's bus was coming, and she would head to the door barking, and then go to the edge of the driveway to meet Jasmine.

Emily also got little treats from Jasmine when I wasn't looking. I remember one day busting Jasmine sharing her snacks with Emily. She enjoyed having her. Unfortunately, for some strange reason Emily had recurring ear infections and things didn't work out. She eventually went back to Canine Assistants, and I'm sure she went on to help another family.

Jasmine was eight years old when she had brain surgery to remove her entire right parietal lobe. It was severely damaged, and the meds weren't helping her at all. She had become ataxic—the loss of the ability to control muscle movement—and unresponsive to meds. The surgery was in two parts. The first part is called mapping, where they cut her open and placed electrodes on her brain to determine where the seizures originated. This procedure was just as dangerous as the actual surgery to remove her damaged lobe. They slowly reduced her medications to help trigger the seizures; this was a seven-day process. Jasmine was having seizures so frequently that they were able to get the mapping done sooner.

The surgical team consisted of a top-notch surgeon named Dr. Shenandoah Robinson, along with Jasmine's neurologist/ epileptologist Dr. Monisha Goyal and her team. They prepared a plan to cut open my daughter's brain once again. I was freaking out, but I had my best friend there with me and she was wonderful. She herself was not feeling well and was scheduled to be checked into the hospital just a few days later. These are the kinds of people that you MUST have in your life through this journey. We have been best friends for fifteen years, and she has helped me in many ways. She was there for Jazz; we took shifts monitoring her.

The surgery took hours, yet it seemed like days, but when it was over this strong little girl—face swollen, head swollen and bandaged, eyes puffy—sat straight up on the bed and asked for pizza. The doctors could not believe it. They were amazed because most children are not even awake for hours following surgery; yet here she was, sitting up asking food. I cried, because no matter what the doctors said she just kept proving them wrong. After the surgery and a few more days in the hospital, we were released to go home. I was too nervous to touch her head; it was soft like pudding. That part of her brain was slowly refilling itself with spinal fluid, and I had to be very careful to not let her fall. She couldn't sustain any kind of head injury for at least six months.

Everyone knows that kids run and do things that cause them to fall down all the time, so I was panicking at every little sound I heard. She eventually got better and went on back to school. Jasmine continued to take her medications—in reduced amounts—for several years. We changed lots of things. I started her on natural and organic supplements, lowered her sugar intake, and included lots of protein in her diet. Every now and then, I still allowed her to have her favorite meal—chicken nuggets and french fries. Her favorite food is chicken and she eats it almost every day.

We later moved to Houston, Texas where we eventually found Texas Children's Hospital and Dr. Angus Wilfong, who is Jasmine's neurologist. The seizures slowly but surely disappeared. Jasmine has been seizure-free for several years and totally medication-free for the last two years. You might be wondering why she had the brain surgery. It was to help her because she was in bad shape! They were hoping that it would stop the seizures, but as always there were no guarantees. I risked it because I knew for a fact that without it, she would only get worse. She was not getting better with medications. In fact she was having more seizures, causing more damage to her brain. Surgery was our only option, although she was not an ideal candidate for this surgery, due to where the seizures originated in her brain.

After having surgery Jasmine continued to take medication for at least five years.—thankfully not as many— with the hope that she would become seizure-free, which she did. It is important that you get the best doctors available to you. Don't take no for an answer, and if the doctor you have fails to meet your needs you should keep moving and searching until you find the best. As I said earlier, I refused to see a resident doctor. I understood this is how they get experience; it is a part of their training so they can become great, like the doctors who treated Jasmine.

I understood that they needed the training, but they were not going to get great learning on my daughter! No offense or disrespect to those resident doctors, I just demanded the best and I found them. Jasmine liked them, I liked them, and they gave their BEST when it came to our needs, questions, and Jasmine's overall care and well-being. The doctors I selected cared, and they earned their positions by being the best. I don't care if you have to get on a waiting list, do whatever is necessary to get the best in that particular field. You never give up. NEVER!

. . . .

CHAPTER 8

Never Give Up and Never Quit!

I want to address a very, very painful subject. So many parents feel guilty because of the condition of their child. I know I did. We often lose focus; we can't concentrate on the littlest things. We want to blame everyone else for our troubles, and we want everyone else to feel our pain. We feel guilty and blame ourselves for their condition. I'm here to tell you what the real deal is according to Tascha. These are my own beliefs, and I hope it helps you to stop feeling this way.

There are many things you may be going through. It doesn't matter if the other parent has left you alone to raise this child on your own, or if they may have moved on and started another family. It doesn't matter if you may wake up every day crying and feeling alone. It doesn't matter if you feel as if you just want to walk away and never look back. Whatever it is you're feeling or thinking, absolutely none of that matters and this is why.... If you walk away and turn your back on your child, what does that say about you?

Do you even care? Did these children ask to be born? Did they tell you to get involved with the other parent and conceive them? Did they have anything to do with the decision you made? No they didn't, so why would you blame them and/or leave them. And yes I said "blame them," because the day you leave and turn your back on them you have essentially made it their fault that they were born!

Did your mother/father walk away from raising you? Maybe one of them did, but the other one didn't; and the one who stayed went on to raise you and make you who you are today. They may not have done the best job according to you, but they did their best with what they had. Oh, I am absolutely positive that you are sitting there saying "I didn't deserve this. I never asked for this." Or you may be asking, "How is it that my friends have children with no disabilities, even though they drank and smoked and everything else?" You're wondering why this happened to you when all you wanted was to be a parent. The world according to GOD does not work that way. He only gives to those he trusts to do this work!

I am going to quote something I read in the 'Woman Thou Art Loosed' edition of the New King James Version Holy Bible by T.D. Jakes. He said, "God made you for His own purposes so that you might reflect a unique aspect of his glory. When you cease to compare yourself with others and refuse to be intimidated by what other people think and say, you are then in the position to birth that business, that ministry, that effort to change your community that God intended. How dare you compare yourself with somebody else! God wanted you to be you. Nobody else, You!"

Now I used that because often times we hope and wish for a normal child, a normal life. (what other people call normal, I should say). But what you don't understand is that God uniquely designed you just the way you are, and He did the same for that child. None of this was done by accident, but it was definitely done on purpose. T.D. Jakes went on to say that "when you begin to compare yourself with another person you are saying, "God, You made a mistake. You failed. You could have done a better job creating me." None of us has the privilege of criticizing God. He is the creator who looks at each of His created beings and says to Himself, "It is good."

So my point is, there is nothing better than what you have now. You have to embrace it. I know that it's hard, I know that it's difficult, and I know you feel alone; but I promise you that on my darkest days I was never alone, and neither are you. I walked away from GOD before; I turned my back on everyone and everything. If they told me anything about the word of GOD, I would run. But something happened! I met some really wonderful and loving people who never gave up on me, and they prayed for me all the time. These people loved my daughter; and they knew that when I was down, it was prayer time. They honestly, with all their heart, loved my daughter and me; and they refused to let us fail. So I hope with each and every word you read, you will know that I refuse to let you fail.

I want you to put yourself in your child's place for a moment. Try to imagine what your child is feeling or thinking. What if you have a child who's in a wheelchair and can't walk, talk, or feed themselves? However, they are very much aware of the people around them; they can see, they can smile, and they cry. Imagine that child wanting so desperately to raise their own hand to their mouth and feed themselves, as they see you do every day. Imagine them wanting to walk around the house as you do, but all day long they have to sit in that wheelchair. Imagine that child wanting to speak words to you, to answer when you speak to them, but they can't. Do you get my point?

Let me help you some more. Your life is not bad, because you have all your faculties and are free to move about at any given time. You can wipe your nose and eyes, brush your teeth, and put on your clothes without the assistance of anyone. You have strength to move your muscles. You can talk and say what it is you want and don't want.

It troubles me when I hear people complain. I used to complain also, but as I started volunteering and helping to coach Special Olympics, my perspective changed. I had the opportunity to interact with so many of the kids who never ever complain, no matter how hard it is. They just smile and keep pressing forward. They have taught me so much.

Understand that it's not wrong to feel what you're feeling. What's wrong is staying depressed and never doing anything to get out of that slump. If you give up, you become a quitter; and you have taught your child to quit as well. You need someone to talk to, i.e. a counselor, psychiatrist, or someone who is willing to listen in a nonjudgmental way. NEVER give up, and ALWAYS keep up the fight! My remedy, which I know will work for you, is to release all of your cares to GOD and He will make it right for you. You may not notice it right away, but you will experience His peace. You may ask him every day when it's going to get better, but I promise you it gets better. It takes time, but it gets better.

I want to encourage you to let go of the hatred and anger in your heart; it will make you bitter and resentful. You will never reach your full potential if you stay there. You will never be able to see the light because you are too busy sitting in the dark. Find people who honestly love and care about you. Ask them to help you, even if it's just for an hour or two. You cannot be afraid to ask for help.

I live a very secluded life, but I do have a select group of people whom I have allowed to be in my life and Jasmine's. They legitimately care about us, and they have our best interest at heart. I want to caution you not to be concerned if the people who are close to you are not your immediate family, as is the case for me.

The people that care the most may not be your family. It is what it is, so accept it. Everyone is not meant to take this journey with you. Do what you must for yourself and your child, with or without them. Just keep moving forward! Most people have no clue, and they aren't trying to get one either. It's a mistake to expect people to do what we think they should do. People will only do what they want to do, and you should not expect them to do anything else. If they don't pitch in to help you, realize that they're not obligated to you.

I learned the hard way when I told my mother, "You never help me with Jasmine." Her response was, "You laid down and had that baby, not me." How do you think I felt when she said that? Did she think I didn't know that, considering that I had pushed her out? My point is, it doesn't matter; you can do this if you just trust and believe you can. You must get to a place where you hold a high opinion of yourself on the basis that God made you and your child exactly, precisely, wonderfully, and uniquely the way you are. You have to know that you were created in the mind of God before you were conceived and implanted in the womb and the same goes for your child. What He did with you, He did with your child. You and your child are His ideas, His creations, and His choices. How do I know that? Because the Bible tells me in Jeremiah 1:5, "Before I formed you in the womb I knew you; before you were born I sanctified you."(NKJV). So let go of negativity; and if you have to walk around pasting post-it notes all around your house to help you with this, do it. I did, every time I had a doubt, I would see one of those post-it notes. I did this for years and sometimes, to this day, I still do. I know that it's not easy; but I know I am not alone, and neither are you.

CHAPTER 9

• • • • • • • •

Sacrifice

THERE are so many sacrifices that you have to make and they are not optional. Don't feel bad about making mistakes along the way, and be prepared to go it alone. Whatever you do, remember it's not about you. You've been given a choice, but with that choice comes sacrifice. You'll have no time, no help, no money, and you sacrifice everything.

People will often stare at your child and never even consider what you may be going through; or how their stares may affect your child. They may even whisper, "What's wrong with them?" or "Why does she look like that?" I remember getting sick and having to retire from my job. At the time, I didn't know that it would give me the results that it did. I was able to be wherever I needed to be at whatever clinic or therapy was necessary. I was able to search out the best doctors; and although I had less money, I had peace because I didn't have to drop my daughter off at daycare anymore. I didn't have to panic every time the phone rang at my job. I didn't have to call in anymore. I was there for Jasmine full time, and I was going to get help.

CHAPTER 10
· · · · · · · · ·

Discipline

THIS will be the hardest chapter for you to accept, because most people don't believe in discipline. Discipline should be part of a meaningful behavior modification strategy and never acted out in anger. Spanking is not to harm a child; it's to make the child better. Stop confusing spanking with abuse. There is a distinction between the two. This is just my opinion; you do what you wish.

I see kids all the time sucking their teeth, hollering, and raising their voices at their parents; and these kids are what they call normal, i.e. no disability. I even see some kids with disabilities doing it as well. Something is clearly wrong with that picture. Somewhere between the child and parent there is a breakdown in communication. Someone has forgotten who is the parent and who is the child.

I remember once while I was talking to my mother, Jasmine did something and I hollered out to her, "NO! Don't do that." My mom said, "Tascha you're so hard on her. She's special needs." That pissed me off. Did she think I didn't know that? I said "Mom, the only need she has is to do what I tell her." I meant that, one-thousand percent. I never allowed her disabilities to stop me from teaching her. It was imperative that I push us to the absolute brink, no turning back. I say "us" because I was being pushed as well. I would not accept what the doctors said. So I did what I knew how.

I knew it was up to me to teach her right from wrong. I knew she understood me, and there was no doubt. I'll give you an example. For a long time she would just say the word "bathroom." She would use one or two word sentences, some sign language, and a lot of hand gestures. There was a time when she was six years old, and she was sitting in the bathroom. My auntie was in town visiting, and I asked her to watch Jazz while I ran to the store. I was gone about fifteen minutes. When I came back, Jazz was still sitting in the bathroom. By this time, she had wiped feces everywhere; it was all over the sink and toilet, and she had even put some in her mouth.

I went into the bathroom, and Jazz just looked at me. She was looking at me because I had been teaching her to wipe herself and flush the toilet. It didn't appear as if she had used the toilet paper. She had decided to play in the feces. Now here is something that a lot of parents with special needs children go through. It has something to do with sensory integration, and the texture of things. I asked Jasmine where the toilet paper was, and she pointed at it. So I knew that she knew to use the toilet paper.

She looked at me and said "Play," and opened up her hands. I said, "No Jasmine, that's nasty." So I knew she understood what she had done. I told her we were going to get a bucket, and we were going to clean that bathroom. I looked up at her and asked her if she had put the feces in her mouth, and she started crying. When Jasmine did things which she knew were bad, she would cry. I spanked her butt right there in the bathroom and told her, "Never ever do that again!" You should always ask for help to wipe your butt and never ever eat that, that's why you sit on the toilet, you wipe and you flush, then it's all gone. Do you understand me?" She said, "Yes, nasty." We cleaned the bathroom, then got her bathed and cleaned up. Never again did she do that. If she needed help she would call me by saying "Help," or she would simply say "Ma."

Most people would ask why I spanked her. I punished her for doing something very bad, and I was raised with the belief that there was nothing wrong with getting a spanking. Sometimes the neighbor would spank you, tell your parents, and then you would get it again; and I turned out knowing right from wrong. I have no problem with discipline. Abuse is something else, and that I don't approve of it at all.

I'll give you another example. One day we were in the grocery store and I had refused Jazz something she wanted, so she knocked the item on the floor. I popped those hands right there in store and made her pick up the items that she knocked over. She never did it again. I remember once she pushed her cousin down, so I pushed her down. She couldn't believe it, neither could her grandmother. I asked her how that felt. Then I told her to never push anyone down. I went on to tell her she should never to put her hands on people, unless someone is trying to hurt you in some way. Did I know for sure if she understood? I didn't, but then again I do not talk to her as if she is disabled. I talk to her normally, and I repeat myself often. I went on to tell her that what she did was not nice, and told her to apologize to her cousin. She walked right over and said, "Sorry." That never happened again either. I used these tactics because it was hard for her to comprehend reading, and she still has trouble writing. So I did more showing and talking, which is how I knew she understood me.

Discipline works when it's accompanied with communication. You cannot discipline with no explanation. I knew she was visual, and I knew she could hear. I did not allow Jasmine to run our house. What I have noticed over the years is that the parents make excuses for their children's behavior. I call it using their handicaps or disabilities as an out. You start explaining away their behavior, never correcting it; and before you know it, your house is upside down. You can't take them anywhere, because you are afraid of how they will act around other people. If you had first corrected the behavior in your house, you would be able to take them anywhere. It makes me mad when I see these children fighting, kicking, talking back, and telling their parents what they are going to do. I don't understand it, and there's nothing anyone can say to make me understand it.

I was at a Special Olympics event with my daughter, and I literally became pissed off watching this child falling out on the floor, fighting her mother, crying, and kicking because she couldn't have her way. I was sick, because I have been doing this for a long time and I am not perfect by any means. However, I do know that a person will do whatever you let them. If you do nothing, this is what you get!

I have watched television programs where the kid is cursing, punching holes in the walls, and fighting their parents. I don't understand how that's possible. But I'll tell you how I believe it happened, and it's okay if you disagree with me. You never got control over your house. You allowed your child to dictate how things were going to run, and you used your child's disability as the excuse necessary to leave you blameless. You gave up!

There comes a time when you must be a parent, which means STOP making excuses. You are not there to be the child's friend. YOU ARE THE PARENT! The Bible tells us In Proverbs 22:6, "Train up a child in the way he should go; And when he is old he will not depart from it." (NKJV) I'm not saying you shouldn't be friendly. I am saying help them, and parent them. Feel sorry later. Get over your guilt, stop worrying, and get busy. Read books about their condition, and don't listen only to the doctors. Get to know your child. Stop worrying about what the doctors tell you your child can't do; start finding out what they *can* do, and build on that.

Stay firm, stay loving, and believe in them; because they believe in you. You cannot be weak. It is up to you and your child to get it, no matter what. I taught Jasmine to say thank you when someone does something for her, to always be thankful. If she did not say thanks, she did not get it. How do I know it worked? The teachers and the other parents—every single one of them—will tell you how absolutely respectful and polite she is, despite being disabled. I very strongly believed that she could do more than the doctors said she could, and these are the results. I get notes all the time from Jasmine's teachers saying things like, "Jasmine is such a joy to have in class," "Jasmine is so polite," and "Jasmine is working hard; she gives it all she's got." I can go on and on, but my point is— Parent.

Discipline is not pleasant for the child or the parent. I didn't enjoy those days, but I look at her now and it was all worth it. The tears, the hurt feelings, you name it. If I hadn't gone through it all, I truly believe she would be doing what I see a lot of children doing—hitting, fighting,, kicking, and slapping their parents, or running off in stores. They holler and scream when they can't have their way, telling their parents to shut up and refusing to obey them. They point at them and stick their fingers in their faces, you name it. I have witnessed all this. I truly believe a lot of these things can be corrected by parenting. That includes discipline, and there is no way around it.

One day at the store, I saw a young lady— who was at least eighteen years old— with her aunt and mother. She was mentally challenged; I watched her walk around the store picking up trash and debris from the floor. I asked her mother, "Ma'am, is she with you?" She replied, "Yes," and I said, "She is going to get hurt. She's picking up stuff off the floor and that thing right there [sic] (it was a metal rod like a shelf hook), she can hurt herself." The lady said, "She is always doing that no matter where we go." Her mother attempted to take the stuff from her, but the young lady screamed and lay down on the floor, or rather the concrete by the door. She was between the door and the concrete, where she could've been hurt, clinging to this metal rod and some other trash she had picked up from the floor. I saw all of this as I was leaving. The aunt was getting the car, and the mother was trying to get her off the ground. She was curled up in a ball, her fist clinched tight, and she was making this humming noise. I put my bags in the car and went over to help her get the young lady off the ground; this took about twenty minutes.

We got her into the car and she started wailing on her mother, smacking her and just swinging away. Her mother tried to get up front in an attempt to get away from her, but the daughter kept hitting her. She was kicking her mother in the back of her head, so the woman had no choice but to get out and return to the back seat. As they drove off, the girl was screaming and swinging. It was a horrible sight to see.

I use this example because although I'm no expert, nor do I have a degree in psychology, nor am I a doctor of any kind, I *am* a mother! I have a little girl (not so little anymore) who's developmentally delayed and mentally challenged, with multiple disabilities. Therefore, I feel that I am capable and knowledgeable enough to speak about disciplining a special needs child. What really gets under my skin, more than anything, is when people who have no children try to give out advice. But that's another book.

Discipline is a very controversial subject. Just recently there was a poll taken; among people who were asked how they felt about spanking, 58 percent approved of it and 42 percent disapproved. In addition, the example used in the poll was a kid who did something which he clearly knew was wrong. The child received a spanking from his dad and later was given a dollar for telling the truth about what he did. The child— who is now a successful grownup doctor— said he never forgot this, and that he crumbled the dollar up. He went on to say that it confused him to be shown love in one instance, and then to be hit.

Here's my take on that example. This kid is now a famous, world renowned doctor with a wonderful, happy family. He's living his God-given life and being of service. If that kid hadn't received a spanking to teach him right from wrong, his life may have turned out very differently. The spanking he received had a lasting impact; he remembered it. Should he have been given a time-out? What a joke! "Please sit me over here in this space, in this chair for a minute so I can think of what to do next." Please! That spanking didn't kill him, nor did it stop him from receiving love. It taught him right from wrong, and as a result he became a very successful adult.

Spanking is a form of discipline. It's meant to be a lasting reminder to a child. It helps the child to remember not to do something wrong again, and that every choice you make comes with good or bad consequences. I guarantee you, my daughter knows —one-thousand percent— that I love her and I'm always there for her; but I will not tolerate inappropriate behavior. There are times when the conversation has to stop. I am not here to discuss and negotiate with the child. I teach, she learns, and we win. I lead the team; I am the parent. That's how I see it. You do what you feel is best for you and your team. So when I saw that poll and heard what that doctor said about his dad disciplining him, I just shook my head. How can he disagree with something that made him better? Understand this, as well. Other people suffer when your child is out of control!

CHAPTER 11

· · · · · · · ·

Puberty

How many times have you said, "I am not ready"? I guarantee I sounded like a broken record. I was petrified. She was slowly becoming a young lady, and her body was changing as she became more curious. I quickly found out that having developmental delays didn't affect her body, which was developing quite normally.

I remember having to explain to her—while shaving her underarms and private parts for the first time—how important it was to always be clean and fresh. "We ladies are not to have hair under our arms." She looked at me like I was crazy; she didn't know what I was talking about. After saying this about three times, I tried something else. I went to the store and bought some foamy shaving cream; and I would put lots of it under her arms, which made it fun for her. It became less intimidating to her.

Along the way, I taught her not to allow anyone to touch her—in any way—except for mom and her doctors. She understood that we were the ones taking care of her and that we would not let anything happen to her.

I taught her by making everything a lesson. I communicated to her while showing her at the same time. When it comes to personal hygiene, it's up to you to make sure your children know how to care for themselves. Once they know, they don't depend on anyone to do it for them, which places them out of harm's way.

Make sure you treat them like young ladies and men when it comes to their physical development. Find the appropriate doctor. Their bodies will go through the normal changes, such as menstruation and breast development, which you went through at their age. It's a good idea to talk with the doctor if you need help dealing with this. I talked to Jasmine and explained things to her. I kept talking, an eventually she got it. How do I know? While getting her ready for bed one night, I was teaching her—once again— how to dispose of sanitary napkins and how to apply them. She did very well and went to bed. When I got up the next morning at the crack of dawn (and I do mean that it was about five o'clock on a Saturday morning), I went to her room to check on her and see why she was up so early. She said, "See ma, I went in the bathroom." She had gone through an entire box of sanitary napkins. It was her understanding that she was to supposed to change them if they became soiled. It didn't matter whether it was a spot or a lot. Needless to say, she must have been up for a while to have gone through a whole box. She had disposed of them properly and everything. The problem was that they didn't need to be changed, and she was not handling the sight of her discharge very well.

I eventually had to make a decision to put her on birth control. I chose the three-month shot called Depo Provera, which helped to control her menstruation. But that wasn't the only reason. I did it because I know I am not always with my daughter; and although I pray that nothing ever happens to her, it's up to me to protect her at any cost. This is a choice you have to make on your own.

There are lots of things to consider. I considered having her sterilized, which would mean a hysterectomy. Why? Because although she is smart and functions well, she cannot take care of a child. You have to make these preparations. You will not live forever, and no one will take care of your child the way you do. So many parents have told me how afraid they are of what could happen with their child in the event of their untimely death or incapacity. Some say that members of their family have even suggested they look into a group home or some sort of living arrangements. Their families have never offered to be their children's caregiver or help in anyway.

This is why I have already prepared for Jasmine's care if something should happen to me. I would never want her to be institutionalized. If she *wants* to live in a group home somewhere with her peers, that's fine. But only if it's her preference, not because she's an inconvenience to someone. You should start thinking and preparing now. It's up to you to make sure your child is cared for. What is a blessing to you is a burden to others. If you don't believe me, ask yourself who has been there with you and your child thus far. Then you decide.

I remember the summer when I asked Jasmine's father to watch her for a couple of weeks so that I could go out of town. He initially agreed; but when it was close to the time for her visit, he told me that he couldn't watch her. I asked why and he said, "Because she has her period and I am not ready for that." Yes, you read it right. I thought I was going to lose it! Was he kidding me? Was her menstrual cycle supposed to stop while he got himself prepared? He also has a wife and two other children, both of whom happen to be girls. I asked him couldn't his wife help him, and he said "It's not her responsibility. This is *my* daughter." Right about now you should be laughing or crying. What a damn joke! Needless to say, Jazz never went for her visit; and I never asked again. I have never forgotten that. As I said before, your blessing may not be a blessing to someone else—even if they did donate an egg or sperm.

Let's get back to puberty; it's time to face reality. I talked with a parent who has a daughter with Down's syndrome. At the time, she was nineteen and had never been taught about shaving her private parts. I was shocked, so I asked her mother why. She said, "She don't [sic] like me to touch her." I replied, asking her "Are you her mom? Are you trying to cause her to have body odor, stuff that you can prevent? What the hell is wrong with you?" I was absolutely pissed. How do you justify not teaching your child the proper way to care for her body. Get over yourself. This is not about you. I will say it until I can't say it anymore. Whatever chance they have at learning starts with you.

CHAPTER 12

• • • • • • • • •

Schooling

It's important that if you see anything that looks suspicious or just doesn't feel right that you ask questions and research for yourself.

I started out in Early Childhood Intervention. I had read books, and I had been around my sister and other friends and family who had children. When Jasmine wasn't sitting up on her own by eight months, and she was crawling backwards with her fist bawled up, I kind of wondered what was going on but didn't know enough. Then she didn't walk until she was 22 months. So there were things that made me ask more questions. That's how I found out about Early Intervention, which lead me to Special Education, IEPs (Individual Education Plan), MFEs (Multi-factored Evaluations), etc. I had to advocate for her rights. I went to meetings, I demanded she be tested, and I never let one teacher give up on her. If you couldn't handle her, then get me another teacher one who could.

Now, this is not to say that the teachers don't do a good job, but truthfully—some don't. I have observed that some of them are just there doing nothing. It's actually quite sad. I often wonder why they have a job, or why they chose to be a special education teacher, considering how much work and patience it takes to help special needs children. I took some time and asked a few teachers, and it amazed me to hear their responses. "We are limited as to what we can do". What does that mean? What are you trying to do? Hopefully teach. I recently went into my daughter's classroom and saw one of her classmates curled up in a corner of the classroom asleep. Somebody, please tell me why this kid is asleep; and the worst part is, every time I have gone it's been the same. He is either sleeping or just waking up. What can he learn while he's asleep? Why is this being allowed? Now, of course the teachers can't discuss another child's condition, but this is just ridiculous. I know that the mother doesn't work. So what is she doing? Why is it so easy for her to just pawn her kid off to the teachers to deal with him? He distracts the other children who are trying very hard to learn. If he's having a problem with sleep, or if he's on medication that causes him to sleep, get some help; but sending him to school and expecting the teachers to deal with him is just wrong on so many levels. It's unfair to the other children in the class, and it's unfair to the teachers. Parents, get involved. Stop handcuffing the teachers. They are there to help your child learn, not to babysit or watch your child sleep.

When Jasmine was about to turn fourteen years old, she was acting up in school. This was when I was first told about this new thing called Attention Deficit Hyperactivity Disorder (ADHD/ADD). This means your child is exhibiting problem behavior, causing a disturbance, having loud outbursts, or is unable to focus. You may have even told your doctor that the child is bouncing off the walls, unmanageable, screaming and yelling, or can't sit still. You know the description.

I found out about this behavioral school and placed her in it. This was very difficult for me. I saw her once a week and brought her home on weekends. She was in the program for three months. Did I like her being away from home? No, I didn't. But no child of mine was going to knock over chairs and bookcases, lay out on the floor in class, or touch people inappropriately. The teachers were calling me saying they couldn't get her off the floor. I would walk into the classroom and there she was, rolling around on the floor; and as soon as she saw me she would jump up off the floor. I knew, again, that she knew right from wrong. This went on for a while. I didn't want them to label her, or be unwilling to help her, which had already started to happen. I mean *really*, you can't get a child off the floor? *Seriously?*

I quickly realized that rather than help her or even deal with her, they would call me. So at least three days a week, I was going to the school. Well, I decided to pull her out of regular school and I put her in a behavioral school. It was the best decision I ever made. Jasmine improved dramatically. I no longer had to go to school; I no longer had to repeat myself over and over.

By this time Jasmine has been placed on ADHD medication, and although she improved and was more manageable, she was also a zombie. She now sat quietly; the inappropriate touching of people had stopped. The school was now reporting all the changes as well. I received reports that Jasmine was no longer running off, she was listening more, she was sleepy, she didn't participate in class, and she wasn't eating her lunch.

I was noticing the same things. We went back to the doctors and they changed her medication, but I still didn't have my daughter. I gradually started weaning her off the medication, and I used the skills they taught at behavioral school to help her. The medication helped to manage all the challenges, outbursts, and acting out behavior, but it also took the joy of out Jasmine.

We struggled, but I just kept pushing her and teaching her. I used the resources available to help her and myself. There are plenty of resources out there; but because no one really talks about it, most parents don't know which questions to ask or even whom to ask. So they just keep giving their children medications, with or without results. We tried everything; however, some things just don't work. Once she was off the medications, she became more alert. All the work we had put in had started to pay off.

There were children who went into the behavioral program at the same time as Jasmine, and they were still there six months later. This was largely due to the fact that I had already been working with her. Again, I went to the classes and I learned how to help her. Some parents didn't even come. Some didn't even pick up their children for the weekend. I was there, I was involved, and that's what it takes.

Jasmine transitioned back into her regular school; the day the school called me and asked if Jasmine's medication had been increased—because she was so alert and focused—I was happy to report that she was no longer on any medication. It was because I took charge and got to know Jasmine even more. I got more involved. I knew it was in there and we fought to get it out.

Education was important; although she couldn't read or write, she could still learn and she did. Oh yeah! I did what most parents do. I bought all the learning tools: hooked on phonics, blocks, letters, cards, you name it. But there was one problem with all that. Home was home, and school was school. Let me explain. One day I set up the dining room with all this stuff and loaded batteries into thee toys, and I was going to help my daughter read and write. After fifteen minutes, Jasmine threw the pencil and book across the floor and—to my surprise—said, "This not school." What had just happened? Did she just throw that book? She put her head down and started crying. I waited for her to stop crying and asked her what was wrong. She just hugged me and said, "All done." I made her pick up her stuff and I let her go to her room.

I later asked her neurologist why she wouldn't color, write, listen to me read a book, or anything like that. That's when I found out that for children like Jasmine, home is their comfort zone; and it's hard for them to put home and school together. If they can't be comfortable at home, it will cause confusion. The doctor said, "Let home be home and school be school." Well that troubled me; because I was supposed to help her learn. But instead, I did just that. I started teaching her things that had to do with home, like how to make her bed, how to fold her clothes and put them away, how to keep her room clean, and how to take care of herself.

I still have to do stuff like wash clothes, mop floors, etc., but I don't have to pick up her clothes. She knows to put them in the basket in the laundry room. She knows how to drain water out of the tub when she's done taking her bath. She knows how to hang up her clothes. She knows where to put her hair stuff. She helps put the laundry away, she helps put the groceries away, and she knows where everything goes. She helps to take out the trash; and she replaces the trash can liners in all of the trash cans. She knows how to refill the toilet paper roll. These things, she learned at home. There are always things to be taught, so let school be school and home be home. She knows how to lather her wash cloth, wash her face, brush her teeth, and hang her towel. She knows how to say grace before she eats and how to say her prayers at night, because these are the things which are important to us! Home is home, and it's where the heart is.

Schools have sports for your child to participate in. They also have Special Olympics, swimming, basketball, baseball, tennis, track and field, and bowling. Get them involved if it's in your area and if your child is able. Make them active, because it gives them a chance to interact with others and to play sports. I was so proud to watch Jasmine play basketball. Not only did she play, she took second place, Silver medal in all events. It encouraged me so much that I got her involved again the next year, and I even became a Special Olympics Coach. It was a wonderful feeling.

There is continuing education, and in most cases your child can stay in school past their eighteenth birthday—some until they are twenty-two years old. Check with the school and the counselors to find out about school-to-work programs. Some colleges have programs for special education as well. You just have to call around and talk to everyone you know. Someone will eventually answer a question you may not have even asked yet, but it will start you on the right path.

CHAPTER 13

· · · · · · · · ·

They're Adults—Guardianship

W HAT happens at the age of 18? You may not have heard of this because I hadn't until I moved to Texas. It's called Guardianship. Here is what I received in Texas:

The definition of Guardianship and Developmentally Disabled Individuals: When a child with disabilities reaches the age of majority, or adulthood (which in most cases is the age of eighteen, but may vary from state to state), it may be time for the child's parent to consider guardianship; because legally, they DO NOT automatically remain their child's natural guardian. It is a decision that should not be taken lightly. In many states, it means that the individual is deemed to be incapacitated and loses all civil rights, including the right to vote, drive or marry. Guardianship is a judicial determination, made in a court of law after an investigation in which the alleged incompetent person may be represented by legal counsel. Because the process of appointing a guardian varies by state, the services of an attorney are often required. In general, the guardian of the person is a fiduciary and is held to the high standards to which all fiduciaries are held in caring for the ward. (Yes, your child is considered a ward of the state). The guardian of the person is required to post a bond in an amount set by the court to assure that the guardian fulfills his or her duties. Unless the guardian's duties are restricted by the court, the guardian is entitled to: have charge and control of the ward, have physical custody of the ward, and establish the ward's domicile. The guardian has the duty of care, control and possession of the ward; and he or she has the duty to provide the ward with clothing, food, medical care, and shelter. The guardian also has the power to consent to medical, psychiatric and surgical treatment. However, the guardian has only limited power to commit the ward to in-patient psychiatric treatment.

Guardianship laws are designed to protect the rights and interests of the ward, and it does so by establishing procedures intended to assure guardian compliance with the rules.

When is guardianship needed? Not all adults with severe disabilities require a guardian. Guardianship is an avenue to pursue only if the person's parents, doctor, psychologist, and caregivers (such as teachers) all agree that the individual is incapable of making informed decisions with appropriate guidance and information.

Guardianship is considered with informed decisions about where a person should live, what care and supervision is required, and how to interact with the medical community. Some states offer limited guardianship in which the guardian is limited in the scope of decision-making. For example, the guardian may have the right to make decisions on medical issues, but not on decisions regarding where a person will live.

The role of the guardian is to enhance the ward's lifestyle while including the ward in the decision-making process as much as possible.

Parents also have to consider who will be their adult child's guardian after they have passed away. It is most helpful to choose an individual who is of the child's generation, perhaps a sibling or a friend of the family. In some states there are non-profit organizations that provide guardianship service.

In many states, parents can designate a substitute guardian (the next guardian) when they cease to be their child's guardian, or they may name someone in their will. For additional information about the state procedures and local services, contact the local area Agency on Aging, the Cerebral Palsy Association, Muscular Dystrophy Association or Head Injury association.

You have to get an attorney and file a lawsuit against your child. In order to gain custody or rights over your child, they must become your legal ward. The above was given to me as I prepared to file for guardianship of Jasmine. I encourage each and every one of you to get an attorney. Do not try to do this on your own. Seek the legal advice of someone who has experience in this field—not just any attorney, but specifically an attorney who deals with guardianship. If you are separated or divorced, the non-custodial parent will need to be served and notified of your intent to gain guardianship of the child or children. Side note here: please check with your state and find out what the laws are for your child in that state.

I thought this was the dumbest thing I had heard of since she is my child, but there is a reason. It's to protect the child's rights, so that no one can take advantage of them legally or financially. Did you know that if you don't do this, your child can refuse to be seen by the doctor? Nor does the doctor have to treat your child, because the child is considered a legal adult. If they say they don't want to see the doctor, you can't force them. It's also a protection plan. I must warn you that it's expensive, so start to prepare.

You will also need to find out, in whatever state you are in, what types of services are available to them now they're adults. There are all types of financial aid, continuing education, and job programs if they can work. Start by talking to the special education diagnostician of the school they attend, and I would start when they are at least sixteen years old, because the process is long. There's a whole list of resources; call them, one by one. Check with the Easter Seals program in your state; they have a wonderful program resource center. Contact the Social Security Administration; they will also be able to help you with your child's entitled benefits. Remember they are eighteen years old now, legally an adult with rights to other benefits due to their disabilities. Talk with other parents where you live and ask them questions specific to your situation. I promise you, if enough of you ask questions of each other and work together, you will find out about all kinds of services, groups, etc. Those services are there to help you with your adult child.

Start doing your research early so that you're not caught off guard. Don't be ashamed. These centers have been put together to help our children; and if we don't use them, they go away and this decreases the resources available. It's about the child; keep that thought first and foremost in your mind.

If they are capable, they can also go to work and there is transportation for that as well. One of the programs here in Texas is Mental Health Mental Retardation Authority (MHMRA). In Ohio it's called Mental Retardation and Developmental Delay (MRDD). So, again, find out what is in your state, go there, and ask for help. It's all about making them as independent as possible.

CHAPTER 14
. . . .
People and Relationships

I made a lot of mistakes along the way. I didn't always do this right. I made a mess of my personal life trying to cope with the pain. I made decisions which I thought were right for me but weren't right for Jasmine. On this journey you'll get lonely, you'll feel like no one cares, and you'll wonder why this happened to you. I caution you to be aware of your thoughts. Be aware of your feelings. Be aware of the people you allow into your life.

There's a saying: "People come into your life for a reason, a season, or a lifetime." What I have found is that when we meet people who are seasonal, we try to make them lifetime. That's not their purpose. That's what you need to know and understand. Stop trying to make people fit into your world. When their time has come and gone, let it be. Take what you have learned from that and apply it to your life. There is always a lesson whatever the subject, be it children, friends or relationships.

If you have people around who do not add to or enhance your life, then why are they there? Is it because you're afraid to be alone? Is it because when they're not there you are alone? Only you know the answer. I know I made some very poor choices out of loneliness, but I also know I made those choices because I did not value *me*. I was depressed, scared and worried all the time; and when you're in that state, you make wrong decisions. I went through beating myself up and the "woe is me" phase, but I moved on and I pressed forward and I learned from those mistakes. I promise if you don't learn from them, or if you keep blinders on, or you start the blame game of what someone else did, you will repeat those mistakes until you get the lesson.

Don't allow your feelings to cloud your judgment. Now, saying that doesn't mean you become judgmental; there is a difference. I'll bet many of you are asking how do you do that. It's easy, because people who really love you and your child will always be there no matter what. They will call, check on you, and offer to help or even relieve you for a couple of hours. They don't ever go away. Those people are lifetime. Then there are people who never return your calls, who claim to be so busy, or—my favorites—claim to have gotten your message but just didn't get a chance to call you back. And just in case I forgot to mention, this is what they tell you weeks later when you eventually hear from them, if at all. I can assure you somewhere in the middle of all those weeks they picked up the phone and called and talked to someone. If they had time to do that, they had time to call you back. My advice is to see it for what it is, not what you want it to be, and let them go. I believe it was Maya Angelou who said, "The first time someone shows you who they are, believe them."

You only need people in your life who love and care about you and your child. If you have ex in-laws, there's a reason for that. Stop trying to be in that family. *You are not*, and that is why they're called "ex"! Have you ever thought about how uncomfortable it makes the new person in that family if you're always trying to hang around and be part of a family to which you don't belong? I'm sorry, but just because you have a child with them, it doesn't make you part of the family. It makes the child a part of that family.

Your child is a part of that family because they are born into it, not because you married into it. And you figure it out when you are no longer married. Blood is—and always will be—thicker than water. Some of you may disagree, and that's fine. I can only speak about what I know. I have talked to several parents of special needs children, and not one has told me different. I didn't say I've talked to all of them, but a lot of them.

It's up to you to lay the foundation for your family. I'm here just to advise you of all that can happen and what to do about it. Take some time and evaluate your life and relationships, then you will get clarity. You have to be open and honest with yourself. If it walks like a duck and sounds like a duck, it more than likely is a duck. Not an ostrich or a penguin—a duck.

I'm telling you if you're not honest, none of this matters. So you're probably asking how you should go about doing this. You pay attention, you move forward one step at a time, and you don't look back. If you're looking backwards, how you can see what's in front of you? Do you have eyes in the back of your head? Forward is the act of progressing, and that's what you are here to do. If it means moving and changing your phone numbers and email addresses, you do that and you move forward.

Get clarity, but be real. "To thine own self be true." I say this because it makes a difference in your child's life and in yours. There's no room for regrets, just action. Get rid of the clutter. You'll know when you have clutter because it consumes you. There's no clarity, you don't sleep, and you are all over the place, lying to yourself. You're confused most of time, and you have no purpose when you're not walking in your God given talents.

Well, how do you know what that is? You don't until you clear out the clutter, then it's revealed in some sort of away. That's how I was able to write this book.

CHAPTER 15

* * * * * * * * *

Taking Care of Yourself

Most people feel bad when they want to get away from it all, and I was no exception. I felt like I was neglecting Jasmine. I also felt resentful, angry, bitter, depressed, and closed off. How many people will tell you that? I can only speak about what I know. I am not professing to be some psychiatrist, psychologist, or teacher. I'm a real person with real feelings. I am a mother of a special needs daughter, I am a single parent, I am a divorcee, and I am a military veteran. These are the things I am sure of.

I went through several years of depression, later diagnosed with Post Traumatic Stress Disorder (PTSD) military trauma. I survived it all, so I guess it's fair to say I am a survivor as well. When it comes to taking care of *you*, it is a must. If you aren't well, then you can't take care of your children properly.

Let me start with depression. Talk to someone; there is absolutely nothing wrong with that. Vent and let it out. As far as medications go, I can only say they didn't work for me. I always felt like I was in a fog.

That's not to say they will or will not work for you. Again, I can't speak on that. All I can say is, there is nothing wrong with getting help. If you are worried about what people are going to say, who gives a shit! They're not walking in your shoes. This is your life and you have control of it. Do what you have to do for you and your family. Unless you are concerned about the people who are running their mouths, then I would advise you adopt the attitude that I had. That attitude was this: unless you are paying my bills, unless you are going to drop everything and come here and take care of my family, then who cares what you say or think? Take care of your own damn house! I say it like that because only you know what works for you—not some outsider looking in.

Not every counselor will work for you. Find someone whom you can talk with. If you don't like that person, find someone else. Take control and settle for nothing less. Learn to rest. I have a pet peeve that will absolutely drive me crazy. I don't like dishes left in the sink at night, so I take care of that before going to bed. I no longer lose sleep if I didn't get all of the laundry done, or if I didn't finish all the house cleaning, or if I got all of the floors mopped except for the kitchen. I don't do that anymore. I've learned to pace myself, make a to-do list, and get done what I can that day.

If you run yourself into the ground, you start to take on these other characteristics like depression, anxiety, worry... do you get my drift? Do what you can do that day and get some rest. If what you didn't get done is not going to cause the world to collapse, your house to fall in, or be detrimental to your child's needs, let it go. I wish I had learned this a long time ago; it would have saved me so much heartache. A restful body and mind helps each day.

If you have a reliable, dependable sitter, use them and get away from it all; and don't feel bad that you did. Go dancing, laugh, and smile because the truth of the matter is this is your life and it will be there when you get back. Go to the spa and get a massage. If money is an issue, start saving. I don't care if it's fifty cents a day. You deserve a break and you should be able to do at least one thing for yourself.

If you have good friends in your life who have helped you and who are REAL friends, they will help you again and not even blink an eye. I remember once, a friend of mine treated me to a Spa Day. She watched Jasmine, gave me a gift certificate, and off I went. You deserve it, so go for it!

If you feel that getting away from it all makes you a bad parent, well I guess I am a bad parent. I am also of sound mind and not on any medications. I'm loved very deeply by my daughter, but most of all I am still standing; and I'm raising the most magnificent, polite, adoring young lady—my daughter! She is thriving and achieving greatness every day.

When you don't take care of yourself, you end up with all kinds of things. Again, I am no doctor, but I can read. Stress is known as the silent killer. It creates tension in your body; it can cause headaches and unexplained illnesses like high blood pressure, etc. I believe many of these things come from not taking care of you. I am not going to get into what you eat and all that. I am just saying do something for yourself. Take care of you and you can take better care of your family.

CHAPTER 16

• • • • • • • • •

The Results

Over the years I have seen all kinds of behaviors, all sorts of medical conditions, and all types of parenting; but what I have seen the most of is Love.

I have spent lots of time talking with all sorts of people including pastors, life coaches, psychologists, psychiatrists, neurologists, and single parents (those with special needs children and those without). I have been in group, occupational, physical, and speech therapies, to name a few. Anyone you can name, it's more than likely that I have talked to one of them.

Sometimes we feel alone, sometimes we don't know what to do, and sometimes we get weary but I am here to tell you we are not alone! When you take the time to listen to your heart, listen to the inner voice that's guiding you, the one that chose you to be this child's parent, you will see life so differently. Now, I call him Savior, Lord, Jesus. You choose what fits you.

But know that you've been chosen; what you do with it is purely up to you. Have you ever heard of free will? It is my belief that the longer you fight it, the longer you stay stuck right where you are. You have a guide; get grounded, get some help, pray, and stop being afraid.

This is what I am sure of. There are millions of parents in this world. But there are only a select few with special needs children. No matter what you believe, this child was not given to you by mistake. You were chosen. You were entrusted to lead, guide and nurture that child. It's not by mistake; it's by design. So when I hear people ask what's wrong with them, my answer is nothing.

There will be hard times when it doesn't seem fair; and although this is the most difficult challenge you may ever face, try putting yourself in the child's place just one time and you will realize that this is not about you. It's not about what's fair and it's not about anything other than the gift that you have been given. God has given you the biggest box under the tree; he has rewarded you. You're probably saying, "Reward?!" –Psalms 127:3 says, "Behold, children are a gift of the Lord. The fruit of the womb is a reward."(NASB) He did this for you and for your child.

There is a lesson here. Someone once said to me, "When the student is ready, the teacher will appear." Never did I think that those words applied to my life. I just thought it had to do with business. But I want everyone to get the lesson.

There is a book that we have all heard of which is the biggest, most sold book in the world. It's called the Holy Bible. If you haven't read it, I encourage each of you to read it. There's a story in there that pertains to your life, I promise you that. There is a homework assignment and a lesson plan in there. It's a guide, it's a resource, and it will get you to your destination. It will—one hundred percent—teach you how to be this child's parent.

Because of the Bible, the Lord, and faith I have come this far to be able to help someone. In this life we don't always understand but we don't have to. Sometimes it makes no sense to you. The key word is "you." It does not have to. If you believe that you were created for a purpose and given life by the Lord, your savior, creator, or whatever you call him, then you will begin to understand that upon creation your life was already planned. You may have done some things along the way that took you off course, but you're here now and you're reading this book. You're searching for answers because you can't get away from this.

Pray, trust, and believe that you are not alone. No more time for depression, crying, and worrying. Make a choice and make a change today. Stop fighting a fight you cannot win; stop wallowing in pity and self doubt and just believe. You don't have to know how it's going to happen, just believe it's going to happen. You don't have to know when it's going to happen; just believe.

My final thought is, this not your child but a child of GOD who you have been asked to take care of, love, and provide for. Do it with honor, do it with pleasure, change the way you think and the way you see it, then watch what happens.

"So now faith, hope, and love abide, these three; but the greatest of these is love! " 1 Corinthians 13:13(ESV).

With Love, Peace and Blessings

Tascha & Jasmine Stith

"We Did It"

My name is Jasmine Stith and I am 18 years old.

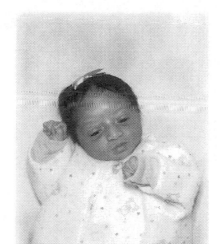

Less than 24 hours old

6 months old

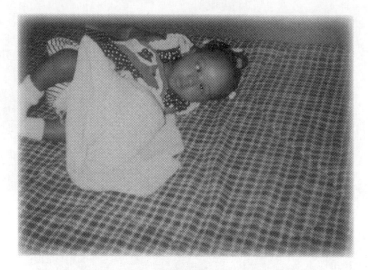

Just prior to my 1st eye surgery

On My 1st Birthday

My first Christmas Picture

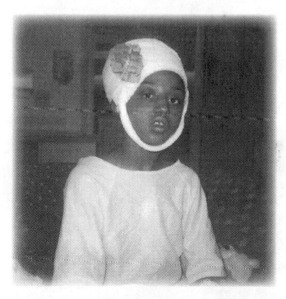

Day 2 - I just had brain surgery to help stop my seizures

Day 3 - after having surgery

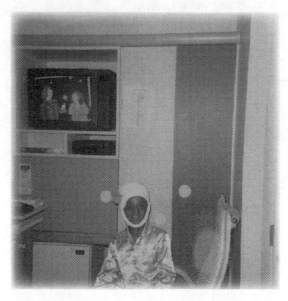

Day 4 - Doing much better today

Emily my service dog, resting

Me and Emily

William Shakespeare – Hamlet

Robert Kiyosaki – Rich Dad, Poor Dad

John C. Maxwell – Teamwork makes a dream work

Dr. Maya Angelou – The first time someone shows you who they are, believe them.

African American Proverb and Dr. Frank Laubach – People come into your life for a reason, a season or a lifetime.

REFERENCES

. . . .

Texas Department of Aging and Disability Services (DADS)
www.dads.state.tx.us

Easter Seals Greater Houston
www.eastersealshouston.org

United Cerebral Palsy of Greater Houston
www.upchouston.org

Texas Children's Hospital
www.texaschildrens.org

Mental Health Mental Retardation Authority (MHMRA)
www.mhmraharris.org

Cuyahoga County Board of Mental Retardation and Developmental
Disabilities
www.cuyahogabdd.org

Brain Injury Association of Texas
www.biatx.org

Tascha L. Stith

Muscular Dystrophy Association
www.mda.org

Shriner Hospital for Children
www.shrinershospitalforchildren.org

University Hospital- Rainbow Babies and Children
www.uhhospitals.org

Texas Parent to Parent
www.txp2p.org

Canine Assistants
www.canineassistants.org